WILD LIFE Watchers

D1098943

Stag Beetle

By Ruth Owen

Educational Consultant:
Dee Reid

Tips for Reading with Your Child

- Set aside at least 10 to 15 minutes each day for reading.

- Find a quiet place to sit with no distractions. Turn off the TV, music and screens.

- Encourage your child to hold the book and turn the pages.

- Before reading begins, look at the pictures together and talk about what you see.

- If the reader gets stuck on a word, try reading to the end of the sentence. Often by reading the word in context, he or she will be able to figure out the unknown word. Looking at the pictures can help, too.

- Words shown in **bold** are explained in the glossary on pages 22–23.

Above all enjoy the time together and make reading fun!

Book Band Orange

For more information about stag beetles go to: www.rubytuesdaybooks.com/wildlifewatchers

What do you know about stag beetles?

How many legs does a stag beetle have?

- 4 legs
- 6 legs
- 8 legs

What is a young stag beetle called?

- A baby beetle
- A chick
- A larva

What does a young stag beetle eat?

- Leaves and flowers
- Chocolate
- Wood

Why do male stag beetles fight?

- They fight over female beetles.
- They fight because they are grumpy.
- They fight over food.

Now read this book and find the answers.

It is autumn in the park.

A tiny animal called a **larva** is eating the wood inside a dead tree trunk.

One day, the larva will change into an adult stag beetle.

larva

A stag beetle is a kind of **insect**.

The larva has mouthparts called **mandibles**.

mandibles

It uses its strong mandibles to bite and chew the wood.

When the larva is hungry it eats the dead wood.

Then it wriggles down into the soil under the tree trunk.

The larva lives under the tree trunk for five years, getting bigger and bigger.

One day, the larva makes a **cocoon** out of soil and wood.

It covers itself in the cocoon.

Then something amazing happens.

cocoon

The larva's body begins to change.

Now it is not a larva any more.

It is a **pupa**.

pupa

Inside its cocoon, the pupa changes into a male stag beetle.

The stag beetle waits in the soil until May or June when it is warmer.

Then he digs up to the surface.

The beetle is 7 centimetres long.

The male beetle has huge mandibles that look like the antlers on a stag.

antlers

mandibles

stag

That is how stag beetles got their name.

Lots of other stag beetles also dig up to the surface.

They are all looking for a mate.

male stag beetle

female stag beetle

wing case

The beetle opens his hard wing cases and unfolds his wings.

He flies off around the park!

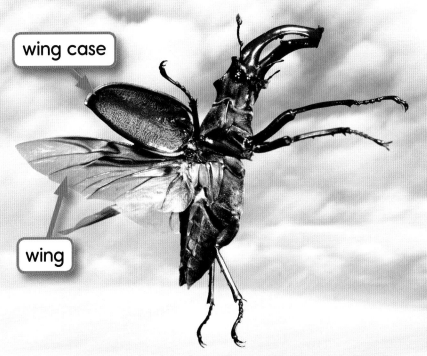

wing case

wing

The beetle chooses an area
to be his **territory**.

He will mate with the females
in his territory.

If another male comes into the stag beetle's territory, there is a fight!

The beetles fight with their huge mandibles.

They don't fight to the death.

They keep on fighting until one of them gives in and walks away.

male stag beetles fighting

The stag beetle doesn't need to eat.

His body still has lots of fat from when he was a larva.

tongue

Sometimes he licks up water or juice from fruits with his furry, orange tongue.

The stag beetle spends his time mating with females.

three males fighting

He also has lots of fights!

A scientist holding a stag beetle.

The stag beetle only lives above ground for about six weeks and then he dies!

After mating, a female stag beetle goes back to where she lived as a larva.

female beetle

She digs down into the soil.

She lays about 20 tiny eggs and then she dies.

A tiny larva hatches from each egg.

The larvae live in the soil and eat dead wood.

larvae

One day, in about five years, they will change into adult stag beetles!

21

Glossary

cocoon
A case in which some insects change from a larva into a pupa and then into an adult.

insect
A small animal with six legs and a body in three parts.

larva
A young animal. The larvae of insects usually have long, fat bodies.

mandibles
The mouthparts of some insects.

pupa
The stage in the life of some insects when they change from larvae into adults.

territory
The place where an animal lives, finds mates or finds its food.

Stag Beetle Quiz

1 Where does the stag beetle larva live?

2 What happens once the larva makes a cocoon?

3 What does an adult male stag beetle do once he comes to the surface?

4 How did stag beetles get their name?

5 Which fact about stag beetles did you like best? Why?